AF207368

the birth date book

This Book Belongs to

Maynard

2003

Love + Hugs
Mom + Walt
xoxoxo

The Birth Date Book

April 16

What Your Birth Date Reveals about You

Stephanie Russell

Illustrated by Claude Martinot

Ariel Books

**Andrews McMeel
Publishing**

Kansas City

CONTENTS

introduction

Your birth date is more than just a passing squiggle on the calendar, more than an excuse to exceed your daily calorie ration. Your birth date is a *fateful* day; a day where the forces of the universe came together in a unique way to chart your destiny; a moment in time imprinted on your very being. Who you are, where you've been, where you're headed—all of these things had their beginning on the month, day, and hour of your birth.

The Birth Date Book sheds some light

on these influences and offers a series of snapshots of who you are. Are you glamorous and outgoing like Cindy Crawford, coolly buttoned-down like Sidney Poitier, or an unpredictable mixture of the two? Why do you prefer a particular color, taste, or scent? What career paths appeal to you? Do you harbor a secret vocation in esoteric anthropology, or does crunching numbers send you into paroxysms of joy? What about your home? Is it styled with the spacious calm of a

Zen monastery or riotously festooned like a Jamaican nightclub? Who can inspire you to drop everything and go to the ends of the earth? And who sends you running lickety-split for the nearest exit?

You'll find both surprising *and* familiar answers to these questions in the following pages. Consider this book a toast to your special day—and to the exceptional being that you are now, and continue to become every day of your life.

your astrological
Sun Sign

ARIES

Aries, the Ram, is the very first sign of the zodiac. As such, it is bursting with energy that simply cannot be contained. Confident, enthusiastic, and independent, persons born under the sign of Aries are prone to rush impulsively into situations . . . and get out before the hard work starts! You are pioneers rather than settlers. While you enjoy rigorous physical or engaging social activities, you don't stay for long.

Your inquisitive nature propels you hastily onward to your next adventure.

You are often said to be headstrong and competitive. You delight in a good fracas, perhaps because your personality is partially shaped by the ruling planet Mars, named for the fearless god of war. You are quick to anger but even quicker to cool off, and your rebelliousness is often equated with courage, passion, and spontaneity.

More comfortable leading than following, you tend to resent those in authority, though you make a good executive yourself. You seek to investigate the unknown and are often impatient with those who lag behind.

Aries is sometimes viewed as the charismatic adolescent of the zodiac. People born under many of the calmer signs will simply stand back in awe at the fiery ways of your take-no-prisoners personality.

your personal
tarot card

your chinese
astrological symbol

THE STAR

The Star is the seventeenth card of the Major Arcana, the twenty-two most powerful cards in the tarot deck. An uplifting image of hope and inspiration, the Star promises that your dreams will blossom if nourished with patience, perseverance, and good faith. Seeds of thought and action you plant now may grow roots far into the future. Break new ground with confidence, and root out the weeds of doubt!

Your sign comes around only once every twelve years in the Chinese zodiac, but during that year your number will definitely come up a winner in the cosmic lottery. Each sign is governed by the qualities of a particular animal guardian. Are you patient as an ox? Wise as a snake? Vain as a monkey? Locate the year of your birth in the chart below to find out—if you dare.

THE YEAR OF THE RAT

1900, 1912, 1924, 1936, 1948, 1960, 1972, 1984, 1996

Popular, ambitious, honest, and stubborn

THE YEAR OF THE OX

1901, 1913, 1925, 1937, 1949, 1961, 1973, 1985, 1997

Patient, strong, original, and rigid

THE YEAR OF THE TIGER

1902, 1914, 1926, 1938,
1950, 1962, 1974, 1986, 1998

Generous, noble, passionate, and hotheaded

THE YEAR OF THE RABBIT

1903, 1915, 1927, 1939,
1951, 1963, 1975, 1987,
1999

Discreet, sensitive, clever, and devious

THE YEAR OF THE DRAGON

1904, 1916, 1928, 1940, 1952, 1964, 1976, 1988, 2000
Enthusiastic, intuitive, shrewd, and demanding

THE YEAR OF THE SNAKE

1905, 1917, 1929, 1941, 1953, 1965, 1977, 1989, 2001
Wise, compassionate, elegant, and extravagant

THE YEAR OF THE HORSE

1906, 1918, 1930, 1942,
1954, 1966, 1978, 1990, 2002
Independent, hardworking, charming, and
rebellious

THE YEAR OF THE GOAT

1907, 1919, 1931, 1943,
1955, 1967, 1979, 1991, 2003
Creative, tasteful, lovable, and fickle

THE YEAR OF THE MONKEY

1908, 1920, 1932, 1944, 1956, 1968, 1980, 1992, 2004

Witty, nimble, passionate, and vain

THE YEAR OF THE ROOSTER

1909, 1921, 1933, 1945, 1957, 1969, 1981, 1993, 2005

Frank, talented, industrious, and pompous

THE YEAR OF THE DOG

1910, 1922, 1934, 1946, 1958,
1970, 1982, 1994, 2006
Loyal, modest, intelligent, and pessimistic

THE YEAR OF THE PIG

1911, 1923, 1935,
1947, 1959, 1971,
1983, 1995, 2007
Honest, sociable, cultured, and gullible

crowning jewel

DIAMOND

Diamonds (from the Greek *adamas,* or "unconquerable") are the most durable gems in the world and have always been linked to everlasting love and marriage. When you wear a diamond, however, you will collect other treasures too. Diamonds are universally hailed as good-luck talismans, and their glittering facets are said to sharpen the intellect and boost the optimistic spirit!

lucky number

EIGHT

Eight is a number of great strength. It is associated with your unique ability to speak your mind—and to have others listen. This is because eights are cosmically tuned to both the present and the future. (The number 8, after all, is simply an infinity sign turned on its side!) Consequently, you are known as a wise planner and a pillar of stability in a changing world.

alphabet soup

I, W, and T

April 16s often find that names and places beginning with the following letters become especially significant during the course of their lives: *I, W,* and *T. Intuition* guides you, *warmth* lights a cozy fire between you and others, and *trendiness* puts you right in step with the pack. (Maybe even ahead!) The latest hot spots and the most adoring crowds are yours for the asking!

week link

WEDNESDAY

Ancient astrologers tied Wednesday to the planet Mercury, which ruled the intellect and the analytical abilities. In mythology, Mercury was the winged messenger who delivered crucial information. Your exceptional "Wednesday-power" combines these eons-old traditions. You may solve complex problems . . . and succinctly communicate the solutions on your most powerful day of the week!

your magical food

POMEGRANATES

April 16s are as full of creative ideas as the pomegranate is filled with seeds. Unlike the velvety-skinned peach or the satin-sheened persimmon, pomegranates are often mottled, lumpy, and asymmetrical. This is not to imply that *you* are unattractive or misshapen, but you *do* sometimes prefer to camouflage your beauty and considerable talents. You get a kick out of taking people by surprise!

your color cue

MIDNIGHT BLUE

For you, nighttime can be the right time. Most April 16s are just coming alive at the bewitching hour (if you're not, you often wish you could be!). Sometimes sly, often secretive, and always intriguing, you are most at ease on the cusp of night. Blue is the color of the spirit, midnight the hour of the soul. No other color could ever enfold you so completely.

flower power

FOXGLOVES

In matters of the heart, April 16s are as welcome as digitalis, the lifesaving heart medicine derived from foxgloves. You are famous for your tender and soft-gloved treatment of those with broken or bruised hearts. But you can be "sly like a fox" too. Throw in some vulnerability and that about sums you up: tender, clever, and vulnerable. In your case, a winning combination!

animal affinity

ZEBRA

Nothing in life is black and white . . . except the zebra! Its crazy stripes perfectly epitomize the union of opposites. It blends the forces of mystery and enlightenment, the known and the unknown, into a sleek, beautiful image with room enough for both. April 16s also possess this unique ability. You allow all "stripes" to coexist without compromising the integrity of any!

ACCOMPLISHMENT

April 16s are always looking for the next challenge—some opportunity to explore possibilities and stimulate a new level of personal growth. Nothing pleases you more than when your efforts produce tangible results. Then you can point to a personal feat and say, "I did that!" with pride.

your secret wish

While you're busily moving moun-
tains and rearranging furniture,
you seem to be having the time of your
life. However, even in the midst of joy-
ously frantic activity, you may hear an
inner voice whispering the unthink-
able: "Relax. Put your feet up. Sip a
milk shake and save Mount Everest for
tomorrow."

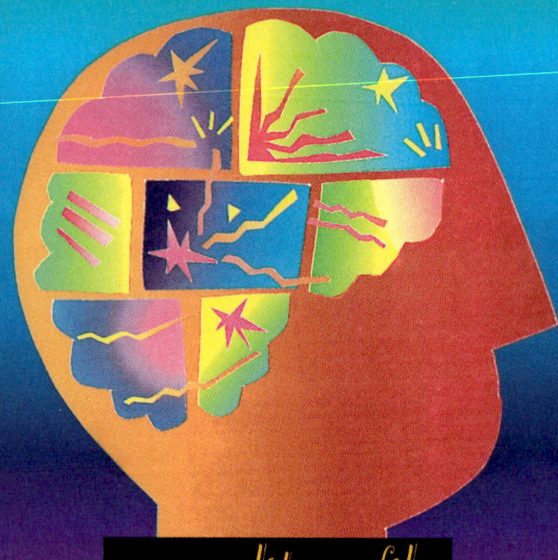

personality profile

Dashing, self-assured, and as power-packed as the express shuttle to Mars, April 16s erupt with good spirit and a healthy dose of old-fashioned spunk. Known for a childlike curiosity and a wide range of interests, dynamic April 16s are generally found smack-dab in the center of any activity—*exactly* where they are bound to feel most at ease.

Swift to anger, and just as swift to forgive, your quicksilver temperament can be as baffling as it is enticing. The range of your moods is indeed broad and intense, abounding with twists and turns that surprise even *you* on occasion. For the most part, April 16s ride the storm of these passions with the ease of a rodeo cowboy. If you *are* thrown off balance, you simply catch your breath, dust off your knees, and climb back on for another round.

Among an April 16's strongest feelings is an unbending loyalty to loved ones. The protective and nurturing side of your character usually doesn't need to be summoned twice, and you rarely balk at the opportunity to do a good deed for a pal.

Giving comes naturally to you, whether it's a cookie and a cup of tea to cheer up a friend, or an afternoon with a wallpaper brush to help your neighbor finish decorating the nursery. In fact, if someone you adore asked for the Moon, you'd personally design, construct, and climb the ladder to pluck it from the sky.

More cautious types generally admire

your forthright, uninhibited manner, although there is a part of you that melts at the sight of a mountain vista or at the innocent antics of an eight-week-old kitten. April 16s are also known to savor the hustle and bustle of busy crowds, which offer both the varied excitement and the occasional cloak of anonymity you crave.

Your nimble mind needs fresh experiences galore to keep it razor sharp. Luckily, you're rarely at a loss when it comes to sniffing out adventures! April

I6s are known for trying out *anything* once, from milking a cow to running with the bulls in Pamplona, Spain!

April I6s know life is short, but it doesn't have to be short on fun!

room for improvement

April 16s often show a practical mechanical aptitude, a natural knack for repairing things and putting them back together in even better shape than they were in before. You most likely take the same no-nonsense approach to self-improvement. In your eyes, it's just like installing the latest upgrade on your computer, or fixing the lawn mower—you want the most power and versatility that your dollar (and a little elbow grease!) can buy.

On occasion, April 16s are good

candidates for the Most Likely to Bruise award—especially if their egos are wounded by some real or imagined slight. In your case, it pays to try to take things a little less seriously—and remember that laughter is the best medicine.

By the same token, your direct, candid style can have a powerful impact . . . but that refreshing honesty can also be unconsciously harsh. It's important to keep in mind that the strength of your opinions can overwhelm others; you might want to try a lighter touch when offering advice.

While many April 16s are cut out for life in the passing lane, there are times when they may suddenly screech to a halt. If you find yourself with some un-scheduled time on your hands, don't be tempted to let it all hang out. Instead, try to pace yourself—perhaps slowing down your breakneck speeds to a canter and speeding up your moseys to a trot!

on the job

April 16s are known to possess a treasure trove of talents . . . and to be somewhat offhand about the range of their abilities. Your powers of persuasion and communication are impressive when you have a goal in mind, and luckily, these skills can be channeled into any number of satisfying, lucrative outlets.

The pace and rhythm of a busy work environment can be attractive to April 16s, who often like to juggle several balls at once. The benefits of teamwork are a good incentive for you, as long as you have your own clearly defined goals to pursue. And, while you operate well within a strict schedule, you also need some flexibility and change in your routine to fight off boredom.

You are often drawn to careers that involve high-pressure situations—corporate sales or law, for example, where you are forced to sink or swim. This kind of position holds your interest and exposes you to a wide assortment of people and ideas.

The fine arts can provide meaningful occupations for expressive April 16s. Careers in art, theater, and music offer both the satisfaction of providing you with endless opportunities to explore your creativity, and the chance to bring pleasure to others as well.

Wherever your career path leads—to business, art, or professional bungee jumping—you will surely use every ounce of energy to make your mark!

at play

Energetic April 16s invest almost as much gusto in leisure time as they do in generating career success. After all, you may reason, all that hard work has to pay off sometime. In your case, it's whenever you choose to call it a day!

Your love of change is apt to keep you on the move, in search of some invigorating new activity to add to your list of diversions. If you are a music lover, your jazz CD collection might have you eyeing that used saxophone at the thrift store and booking lessons with a local alto player. The potted tea rose your sister sent might unlock a hidden ambition to cultivate exotic blooms. With April 16s, a simple glimpse of beauty can easily become a hobby or even a lifetime passion.

If you are drawn to the outdoors, there's a good chance you might end up parasailing on Chesapeake Bay or parachuting in the Catskills . . . anything that gives you an exhilarating boost. Adventurous April 16s like taking risks and challenging their own fears. On some days, this might mean diving into the deep end of the pool, where you might encounter a wild, inflatable sea-horse—but with your imagination, that can be *plenty* of excitement!

While April 16s may find joy in the strobe light of a dance floor, or in a downhill bicycle race at bone-chilling speed, they can find as much pleasure in their own backyard playing Frisbee with their dog, their sister, or that new guy down the street who makes such great iced tea.

home sweet home

Walking into an April 16's home can be like entering a workshop where elves toil away at everything from toy making to cookie-baking. An atmosphere of pleasant commotion may prevail where various projects and domestic clutter coexist like old friends who don't need to put on a tie for dinner.

Many April 16s treasure their homes as places to indulge and enjoy every whim . . . from building an antique headlight collection to publishing a personal recipe newsletter. You may *try* to keep everything in its place, but inevitably, one activity spills over into another; as you stroll, chatting on the portable phone, the soup ladle might end up *anywhere* between the model airplane table and the laundry room.

A variety of people traipse through your foyer, from the neighbor's kids to various friends and associates to your cousin, the reptile veterinarian. You are the type to leave out cookies and milk and a pinochle deck, while weaving between the houseguests and your fax machine. In fact, your place might be a kind of fun house rest stop for people where they can kick off their tennis shoes and relax in the friendly chaos of your sanctuary.

On occasion, you are capable of closing the door gently but firmly and taking a rare break from the world. During those hours, you gather your resources and, feet up and club soda in hand, you take a much-needed breather from your merry-go-round social schedule.

how do you love?

R omantic, and as impulsive as carefree children, April 16s simply *live* for passion. Your heartstrings are always aching to be plucked by a mate who shares your devotion to the time-honored art of love.

Popular April 16s often walk around with a dance card that has several candidates scribbled in. And for a while, you might enjoy the free-spirited fun of promenading about with any number of interesting prospects on your arm. But beneath your happy-go-lucky exterior is a need for real, lasting togetherness with a special someone.

When you *do* meet your true love, it's as if an automatic valve kicks open to release a geyser of untapped emotion . . . and your lucky partner becomes the willing recipient of a lifetime's worth of affection. There's no end to the lavish warmth you're capable of bestowing on a loved one—from steamy, ravenous attentions to quiet, gentle moments of intimacy and support.

In return, April 16s' needs are simple:

a listening ear, a tender touch, and a loyalty as fierce as their own. That allegiance is the tie that binds you and your partner through the rockiest bits of any relationship. That, and a shared craving for chocolate, can pull you through just about any crisis! In the end, your willingness to share—thoughts, feelings (*and* his-and-her éclairs)—will forge that enduring bond you've always desired.

whom do you love?

April 16s (Aries) get along best
with:

Aries (March 21–April 20)
Gemini (May 22–June 21)
Leo (July 24–August 23)
Capricorn
   (December 22–January 20)
Aquarius (January 21–February 19)
Pisces (February 20–March 20)

April 16s (Aries) get along better
without:

Taurus (April 21–May 21)
Cancer (June 22–July 23)
Virgo (August 24–September 23)
Libra (September 24–October 23)
Scorpio (October 24–November 22)
Sagittarius
    (November 23–December 21)

April 16s seek out people who are:

exciting, confident, hopeful, complex, unselfish, and adventurous.

April 16s avoid people who are:

possessive, bossy, demanding, shrill, self-absorbed, or insincere.

famous/infamous people born today

Ellen Barkin (1955) actress, *The Big Easy, Sea of Love*

Clifford Case (1904) senator from New Jersey

Fran Robinson (1970) actress, *Charlie & Company*

Kareem Abdul-Jabbar (1947) basketball center, Los Angeles Lakers

Wilbur Wright (1867) aviation pioneer

Kingsley Amis (1922) novelist and poet,
Lucky Jim

Merce Cunningham (1919) modern dancer
and choreographer, *Suite by Chance*

Gerardo (1965) rapper, "Rico Suave"

Charlie Chaplin (1889) comic actor and
director, *The Gold Rush, Modern Times;*
the Little Tramp

John II (1319) king of France

Lukas Haas (1976) actor, *Witness,*
Rambling Rose

Herbie Mann (1930) jazz flutist and
saxophonist

APRIL 16

New York Yankees become the first baseball team to put numbers on their uniforms (1929)

Chemist Albert Hofmann, creator of LSD, accidentally takes the first "trip" when a small amount is absorbed through the skin of his finger (1943)

Walter Cronkite debuts as anchor of *The CBS Evening News* (1962)

flashback: your past lives

In any past life, April 16s would have been in close connection to fire—or its symbolic equivalent, creativity. It is not unlikely that your past lives included the following occupations:

Firefighter
Novelist
Welder
Barbecue chef
Burn-unit nurse
Composer

A trout in the pot is worth two salmon in the sea.

Irish proverb

a word of advice

Everyone admires the ease with which you juggle getting things done—putting out fires and tap-dancing your merry way to fulfillment. You create a dazzling show, but in the long run, it pays to heed your inner voice and slow down. Take time to not only smell the flowers, but also those rich coffee beans, the rain in the air, or a slowly-burning scented candle.

looking ahead

Gazing into the future and visualizing the ideal image of your life-to-be can be tricky for someone like you, who lives so intensely in the moment. Still, you have all the creative vision needed to form a splendid and attainable conception of who you wish to become—and perhaps most important, the road you'll take to get there.